Guinea Pigs and Rabbits

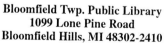

CHELSEA CLUBHOUSE

An Imprint of Chelsea House Publishers
A Haights Cross Communications Company

Philadelphia

June Loves

This edition first published in 2004 in the United States of America by Chelsea Clubhouse, a division of Chelsea House Publishers and a subsidiary of Haights Cross Communications.

Chelsea Clubhouse
1974 Sproul Road, Suite 400
Broomall, PA 19008-0914

The Chelsea House world wide web address is www.chelseahouse.com

Library of Congress Cataloging-in-Publication Data

Loves, June.
  Guinea pigs and rabbits / June Loves.
    v. cm. — (Pets)

Contents: Guinea pigs and rabbits — Kinds of guinea pigs — Kinds of rabbits — Parts of a guinea pig — Parts of a rabbit — Young guinea pigs — Young rabbits — Choosing guinea pigs and rabbits — Caring for guinea pigs and rabbits — Cleaning — Feeding — Grooming — Handling — Training — Visiting the vet — Pet clubs — In the wild.

  ISBN 0-7910-7552-4
  1. Guinea pigs as pets—Juvenile literature. 2. Rabbits—Juvenile literature. [1. Guinea pigs.
  2. Rabbits as pets. 3. Pets.] I. Title. II. Series.
  SF459.G9 L68 2004
  636.9'322—dc21

                                                                    2002155670

First published in 2003 by
MACMILLAN EDUCATION AUSTRALIA PTY LTD
627 Chapel Street, South Yarra, Australia, 3141

Associated companies and representatives throughout the world.

Copyright © June Loves 2003
Copyright in photographs © individual photographers as credited

Page layout by Domenic Lauricella
Photo research by Legend Images

Printed in China

Acknowledgements
The author and the publisher are grateful to the following for permission to reproduce copyright material:

Cover photographs: girl with pet guinea pig and boy with pet rabbit, courtesy of Getty Images.

ANT Photo Library, pp. 11, 30 (bottom); © Ken Lucas/Ardea London Limited, p. 30 (top); Michel Gunther—Bios/Auscape, p. 22; Dominique Halleux—Bios/Auscape, p. 9 (main); C. Andrew Henley/Auscape, p. 7; Nigel Clements, p. 28; Coo-ee Picture Library, p. 12; The DW Stock Picture Library, p. 24; Getty Images, pp. 1, 8 (main), 25, 27; Legend Images, pp. 14–15; MEA Photo, p. 15 (toys and brushes); Pelusey Photography, pp. 5, 16–17, 19, 23; Photography Ebiz, pp. 4, 6, 8 (teeth), 9 (teeth), 10, 13, 18, 29; Dale Mann/Retrospect, pp. 20, 21, 26.

With special thanks to the Tunstall Square Pet Shop and The Pines Pet Centre, The Ark.

While every care has been taken to trace and acknowledge copyright, the publisher tenders their apologies for any accidental infringement where copyright has proved untraceable. Where the attempt has been unsuccessful, the publisher welcomes information that would redress the situation.

Contents

Guinea Pigs and Rabbits 4

Kinds of Guinea Pigs 6

Kinds of Rabbits 7

Parts of a Guinea Pig 8

Parts of a Rabbit 9

Young Guinea Pigs 10

Young Rabbits 11

Choosing Guinea Pigs and Rabbits 12

Caring for Guinea Pigs and Rabbits 14

Cleaning 20

Feeding 22

Grooming 24

Handling 25

Training 26

Visiting the Vet 28

Pet Clubs 29

In the Wild 30

Glossary 31

Index 32

Guinea Pigs and Rabbits

Guinea pigs and rabbits are quiet, gentle pets. They live in **hutches**. Guinea pigs and rabbits need plenty of space to move about.

Guinea pigs are small and furry.

Rabbits have long ears.

Guinea pigs and rabbits can live indoors. They may be taken outside when the weather is warm, but not hot. They need exercise and care every day.

Kinds of Guinea Pigs

There are many **breeds** of guinea pigs. They can have different kinds and colors of fur.

- Smooth-haired guinea pigs have smooth, short fur.
- Long-haired guinea pigs have long, silky fur.
- Rough-haired guinea pigs have fur that swirls and curls.

Abyssinian guinea pigs are rough-haired guinea pigs.

Kinds of Rabbits

There are many breeds of rabbits. They can be different sizes and colors. Their fur can be different lengths.

- Albino rabbits have white fur and pink eyes.
- Angora rabbits have long, fluffy fur.
- Lop rabbits have ears that hang down beside their face.
- Rex rabbits have velvety coats.

Albino rabbits are popular pets.

Parts of a Guinea Pig

A guinea pig is a **mammal**. Guinea pigs have short ears and no tails.

chisel-shaped
teeth for gnawing

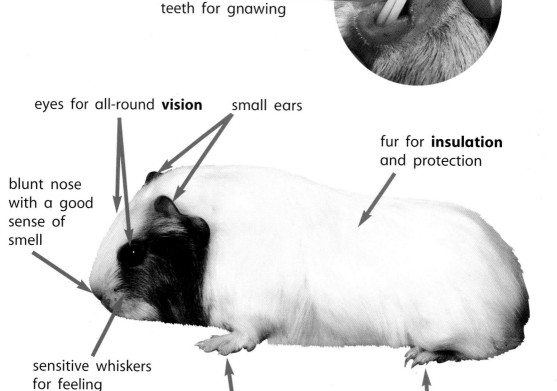

eyes for all-round **vision**   small ears

fur for **insulation**
and protection

blunt nose
with a good
sense of
smell

sensitive whiskers
for feeling

short front legs
with four claws

longer back legs
with three claws

Parts of a Rabbit

A rabbit also is a mammal. Rabbits have long ears and short tails.

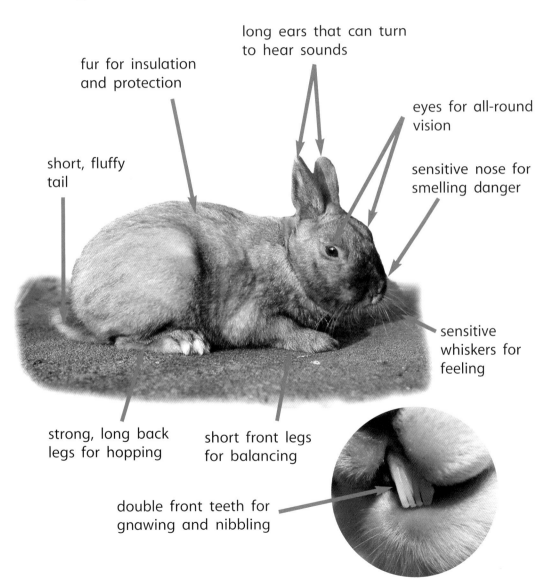

long ears that can turn to hear sounds

fur for insulation and protection

eyes for all-round vision

short, fluffy tail

sensitive nose for smelling danger

sensitive whiskers for feeling

strong, long back legs for hopping

short front legs for balancing

double front teeth for gnawing and nibbling

Young Guinea Pigs

Female guinea pigs usually have two to five young in a **litter**. Young guinea pigs are called pups. They are born with all their fur and their eyes open. Guinea pig pups feed on their mother's milk for three weeks. They quickly learn to eat solid food.

Young guinea pigs can move around when they are one week old.

Young Rabbits

Female rabbits usually have four to twelve young in a litter. Young rabbits are called kittens. They are born without fur and their eyes shut. Young rabbits feed on their mother's milk for six to eight weeks.

Young rabbits are helpless at birth.

Choosing Guinea Pigs and Rabbits

Choose pet guinea pigs and rabbits with shiny fur, clean noses, clean ears, and bright eyes. Choose healthy pets that move well.

Another name for a guinea pig is a cavy.

You may adopt adults or young animals. Guinea pig pups should be at least six to eight weeks old. Rabbit kittens should be at least eight to ten weeks old.

Animal shelters have many animals that need homes.

Caring for Guinea Pigs and Rabbits

Guinea pigs and rabbits need a similar kind of home. These are some of the supplies you may want to care for your pet guinea pig or rabbit.

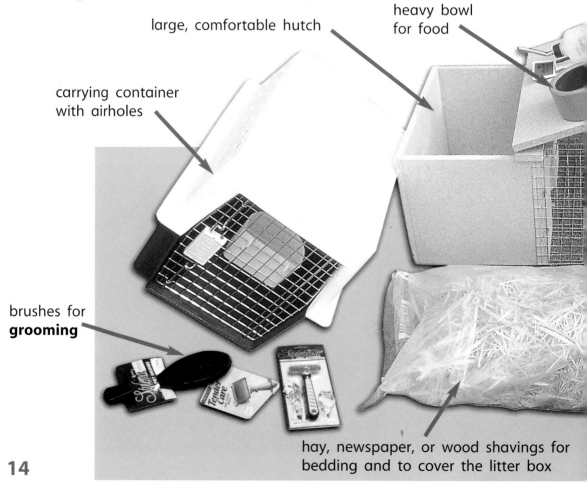

large, comfortable hutch

heavy bowl for food

carrying container with airholes

brushes for **grooming**

hay, newspaper, or wood shavings for bedding and to cover the litter box

A piece of natural wood for chewing will stop your pet's teeth from growing too long.

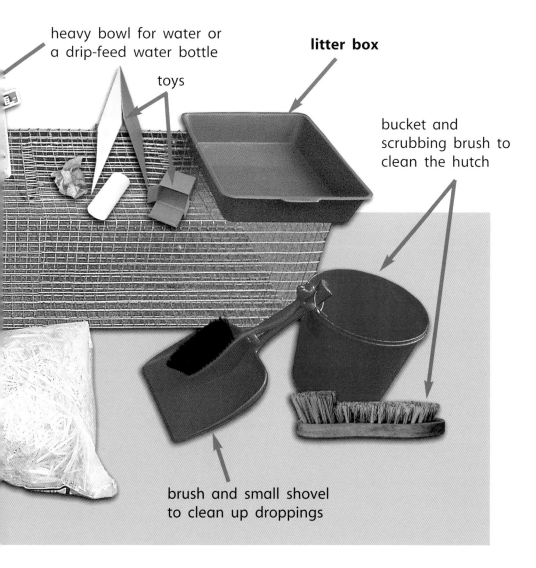

heavy bowl for water or
a drip-feed water bottle

litter box

toys

bucket and
scrubbing brush to
clean the hutch

brush and small shovel
to clean up droppings

The hutch

Guinea pigs and rabbits need a hutch to live in. The hutch needs to be safe, easy to clean, and weatherproof.

a small, dark area for sleeping

straw, wood shavings, or paper for bedding

Indoor hutches need to be enclosed and off the ground. Place them away from drafts and heaters.

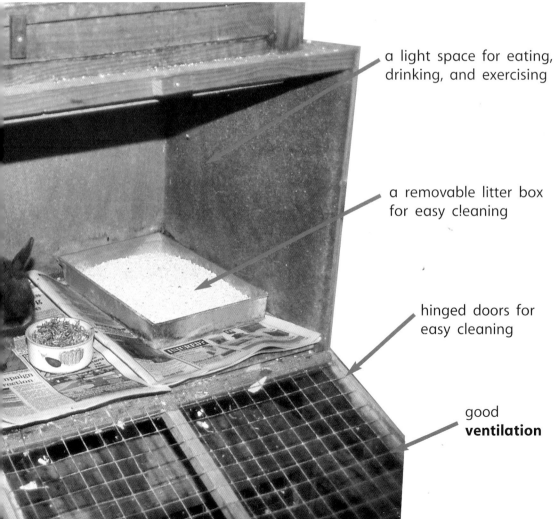

a light space for eating, drinking, and exercising

a removable litter box for easy cleaning

hinged doors for easy cleaning

good **ventilation**

Guinea pigs and rabbits can be outdoors in mild weather. An outdoor run should have a mesh fence on the sides, top, and bottom.

Pets can be outside in warm, but not hot, weather.

An outdoor run can be moved from one part of the yard to another. Guinea pigs and rabbits like new grass to **graze** on and a different exercise area.

This outdoor run has lots of space for the rabbit to exercise.

Cleaning

It is important to keep your pets' home clean.

The litter box

⚙ Wash and clean your pets' litter box
every day.

⚙ Replace the litter.

Food and water containers

⚙ Clean food and water
containers every day.

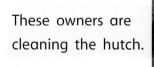

These owners are
cleaning the hutch.

The hutch

Make sure your pets are safe while you clean their hutch.

- ❂ Take out dirty bedding and uneaten food every day.
- ❂ Clean and scrub the hutch once a week with warm, soapy water.
- ❂ Rinse and dry the hutch well.
- ❂ Replace the bedding, food, and water.

Hay makes good bedding.

Feeding

Guinea pigs and rabbits need to be fed every day. You can buy guinea pig or rabbit pellets from a pet store or supermarket. Guinea pigs and rabbits also need hay to nibble.

Guinea pigs and rabbits eat throughout the day.

Treat your pets to small amounts of fresh fruit, leafy vegetables, and **root vegetables** every day. Guinea pigs and rabbits also need clean, fresh water every day.

Carrots are a root vegetable that rabbits eat.

Grooming

Combing and brushing removes loose, dead hair. This helps to keep your pet healthy.

Rabbits with long hair need brushing every day to keep their fur tangle-free.

Handling

Handle guinea pigs and rabbits gently. Lift them up by the back of their neck with one hand, and support their **hindquarters** with the other hand. Loud noises and sudden movements frighten guinea pigs and rabbits.

Hold a guinea pig against your chest to make it feel safe.

25

Training

You can train pet guinea pigs and rabbits to wet and leave their droppings in a litter box. Use food or praise as rewards to train your pets.

You can train your rabbit to eat from your hand.

Guinea pigs and rabbits can be tamed easily when they are young. A guinea pig can learn to greet you with a high-pitched squeal. Spend time with your pet every day.

Rabbits need attention every day.

Visiting the Vet

If your guinea pig or rabbit does not seem well, take it to the **vet** for advice and treatment. A regular check with the vet will keep your pet healthy. The vet can check if your guinea pig's teeth and claws have grown too long.

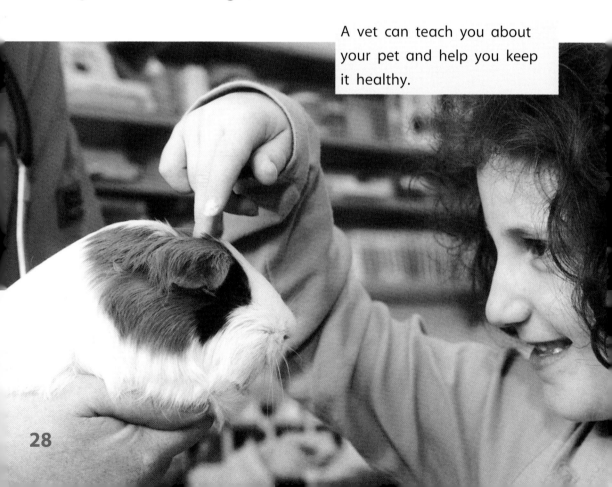

A vet can teach you about your pet and help you keep it healthy.

Pet Clubs

Many guinea pig and rabbit owners join pet clubs. They may enter their pets in competitions and share information.

Judges may award prizes to the pet with the best features.

In the Wild

Wild guinea pigs live in South America in big family groups. They sleep and find shelter under logs or in caves and burrows. Wild rabbits live in many places around the world. They live in underground burrows.

Wild guinea pigs live in South America.

Wild rabbits live in many areas of the world.

Glossary

breeds	animals that belong to the same scientific group and have a similar appearance
graze	to feed on grass
grooming	brushing or combing a pet to keep it clean
hindquarters	the back part of an animal
hutches	larger cages or pens for some types of animals
insulation	a way of keeping heat and cold in or out
litter	animals born at the same time to the same mother; also, a material used in a litter box to absorb an animal's waste and droppings
litter box	a tray where pets can wet and leave their droppings
mammal	a warm-blooded animal covered with hair whose young feed on their mother's milk
root vegetables	vegetables with roots you can eat, such as carrots and parsnips
ventilation	a way of letting plenty of air into a place
vet	a doctor who treats animals; short for veterinarian
vision	ability to see

Index

a
albino rabbits 7
Angora rabbits 7
b
bedding 14, 16, 21
breeds 6–7
c
carrying container 14
cleaning 15, 16, 17, 20–21
clubs 29
competitions 29
e
exercise 5, 19
f
feeding 22–23
food 10, 11, 19, 21, 22–23, 26
food container 14, 20
g
grooming 14, 24
h
handling 25
hutches 4, 14, 16–17, 21
k
kinds of guinea pigs 6
kinds of rabbits 7
kittens 11

l
litter box 14, 15, 17, 20, 26
long-haired guinea pigs 6
lop rabbits 7
o
outdoor run 18–19
p
parts of a guinea pig 8
parts of a rabbit 9
pups 10
r
rex rabbits 7
rough-haired guinea pigs 6
s
smooth-haired guinea pigs 6
t
taming 27
toys 15
training 26
v
vet 28
w
water 21, 23
water container 15, 20
wild guinea pigs and rabbits 30
y
young guinea pigs 10
young rabbits 11